AF882493

# To Become an Oracle® DBA

# In Eighty Days

By

Fly Balloon

Copyright © 2007 by Fly Balloon

*All rights reserved. No part of this book shall be reproduced or transmitted in any form or by any means, electronic, mechanical, magnetic, photographic including photocopying, recording or by any information storage and retrieval system, without prior written permission of the publisher. No patent liability is assumed with respect to the use of the information contained herein. Although every precaution has been taken in the preparation of this book, the publisher and author assume no responsibility for errors or omissions. Neither is any liability assumed for damages resulting from the use of the information contained herein.*

ISBN 978-0-7414-3819-5

Published by:

INFINITY
PUBLISHING.COM

1094 New Dehaven Street, Suite 100
West Conshohocken, PA 19428-2713
Info@buybooksontheweb.com
www.buybooksontheweb.com
Toll-free (877) BUY BOOK
Local Phone (610) 941-9999
Fax (610) 941-9959

*Printed in the United States of America*

*Published January 2014*

# PREFACE

Hello everyone, this is Fly Balloon, from Singapore, a tiny tropical island, which has been described by Jules Verne in his great novel <<Around the World in 80 Days>> in 19th century as thus:

"Pepper plants replaced the prickly hedges of European fields; sago-bushes, large ferns with gorgeous branches, varied the aspect of this tropical clime; while nutmeg-trees in full foliage filled the air with a penetrating perfume. Agile and grinning bands of monkeys skipped about in the trees, nor were tigers wanting in the jungles."

Now there is no more monkey and tiger wanting around; the pepper plants were replaced by concrete forest, inside which live some intelligent creatures such as DBAs. Fogg is one of them, as a fan of Jules Verne, he is always dreaming to explore the experience of traveling around world in most natural and ancient ways. One day with his perfect database skill he managed to connect to the matrix database and issue a recover command, amazingly, the time return back to a hundred years ago...

*Mr. Phileas Fogg lived, in 1872, at No. 7, Saville Row, Burlington Gardens. At half-past eleven in the morning, he reached the Reform Club where his usual partners at whist for the Standard: andrew Stuart, an engineer; John Sullivan and Samuel Fallentin, bankers; Thomas Flanagan, a brewer; and Gauthier Ralph, one of the Directors of the Bank of England.*

*"Well, Ralph," said Thomas Flanagan, "what about that robbery?"*

*"Oh," replied Stuart, "the Bank will lose the money."*

*"On the contrary," broke in Ralph, "I hope we may put our hands on the robber. Skilful detectives have been sent to all the principal ports of America and the Continent."*

*The affair which formed its subject, and which was town talk, had occurred three days before at the Bank of England. A package of banknotes, to the value of fifty-five thousand pounds, had been taken from the principal cashier's table, that functionary being at the moment engaged in registering the receipt of three shillings and sixpence. Of course, he could not have his eyes everywhere.*

*"Well, where can he fly to?" asked Ralph. "No country is safe for him."*

*"Oh, I don't know that. The world is big enough."*

*The incredulous Stuart was not convinced, and when the hand was finished, said eagerly: "You have a strange way, Ralph, of proving that the world has grown smaller. So, because you can go round it in three months--"*

*"In eighty days," interrupted Phileas Fogg.*

*"That is true, gentlemen," added John Sullivan. "Only eighty days, now that the section between Rothal and Allahabad, on the Great Indian Peninsula Railway, has been opened. Here is the estimate made by the Daily Telegraph:*

*From London to Suez via Mont Cenis and Brindisi, by rail and steamboats ................ 7 days*
*From Suez to Bombay, by steamer ................... 13 "*
*From Bombay to Calcutta, by rail .................. 3 "*
*From Calcutta to Hong Kong, by steamer ............ 13 "*
*From Hong Kong to Yokohama (Japan), by steamer ..... 6 "*
*From Yokohama to San Francisco, by steamer ......... 22 "*
*From San Francisco to New York, by rail ............ 7 "*
*From New York to London, by steamer and rail ........ 9 "*
----
*Total ........................................... 80 days."*

*"Yes, in eighty days!" exclaimed Stuart, who in his excitement made a false deal. "But that doesn't take into account bad weather, contrary winds, shipwrecks, railway accidents, and so on."*

*"Quite possible," returned Mr. Fogg.*

*"The journey round the world in eighty days?"*

*"A true Englishman doesn't joke when he is talking about so serious a thing as a wager," replied Phileas Fogg, solemnly. "I will bet twenty thousand pounds against anyone who wishes that I will make the tour of the world in eighty days or less; Do you accept?"*

*"We accept," replied Messrs. Stuart, Fallentin, Sullivan, Flanagan, and Ralph, after consulting each other.*

*"Good," said Mr. Fogg. "The train leaves for Dover at a quarter before nine. I will take it."*

*– From Jules Verne, <<Around the World in 80 Days>>*

# CONTENTS

# Chapter One Oracle Database Architecture

Fogg decided to travel the world by hot air balloon in order to speed up the journey. Passepartout was excited about the decision and worked hard to load fuel and food into the basket. However, the basket had weight limitation and cannot load with too much water. The French young man showed up his talent by invented a condensing pipe which can extract water from vapor in atmosphere.

Fogg in the meantime, found no time to help Passepartout but dedicated himself to learn Geography and Meteorology at the last minute and currently was concentrating on a world water circulation map.

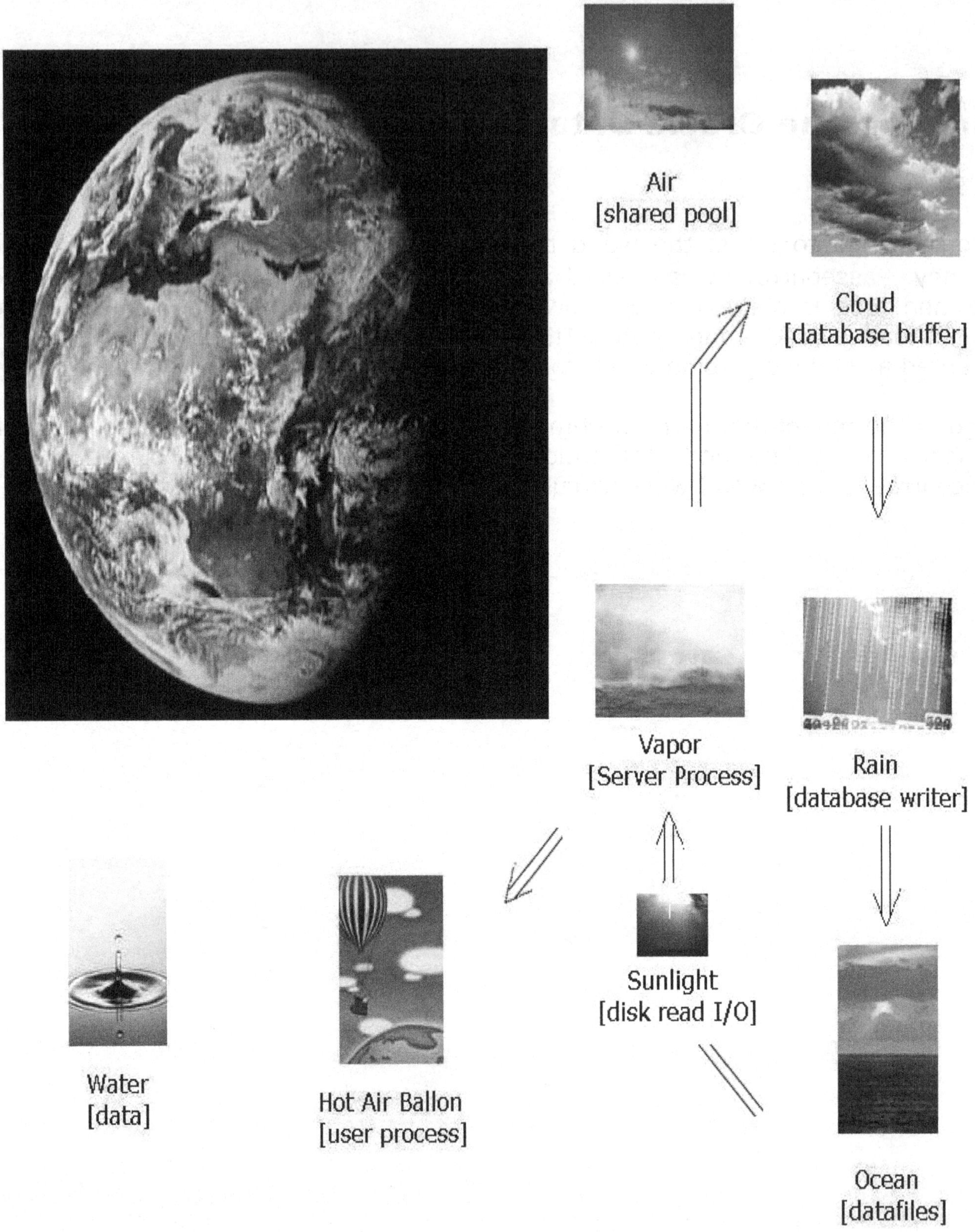
Air
[shared pool]
Cloud
[database buffer]
Vapor
[Server Process]
Rain
[database writer]
Water
[data]
Hot Air Ballon
[user process]
Sunlight
[disk read I/O]
Ocean
[datafiles]

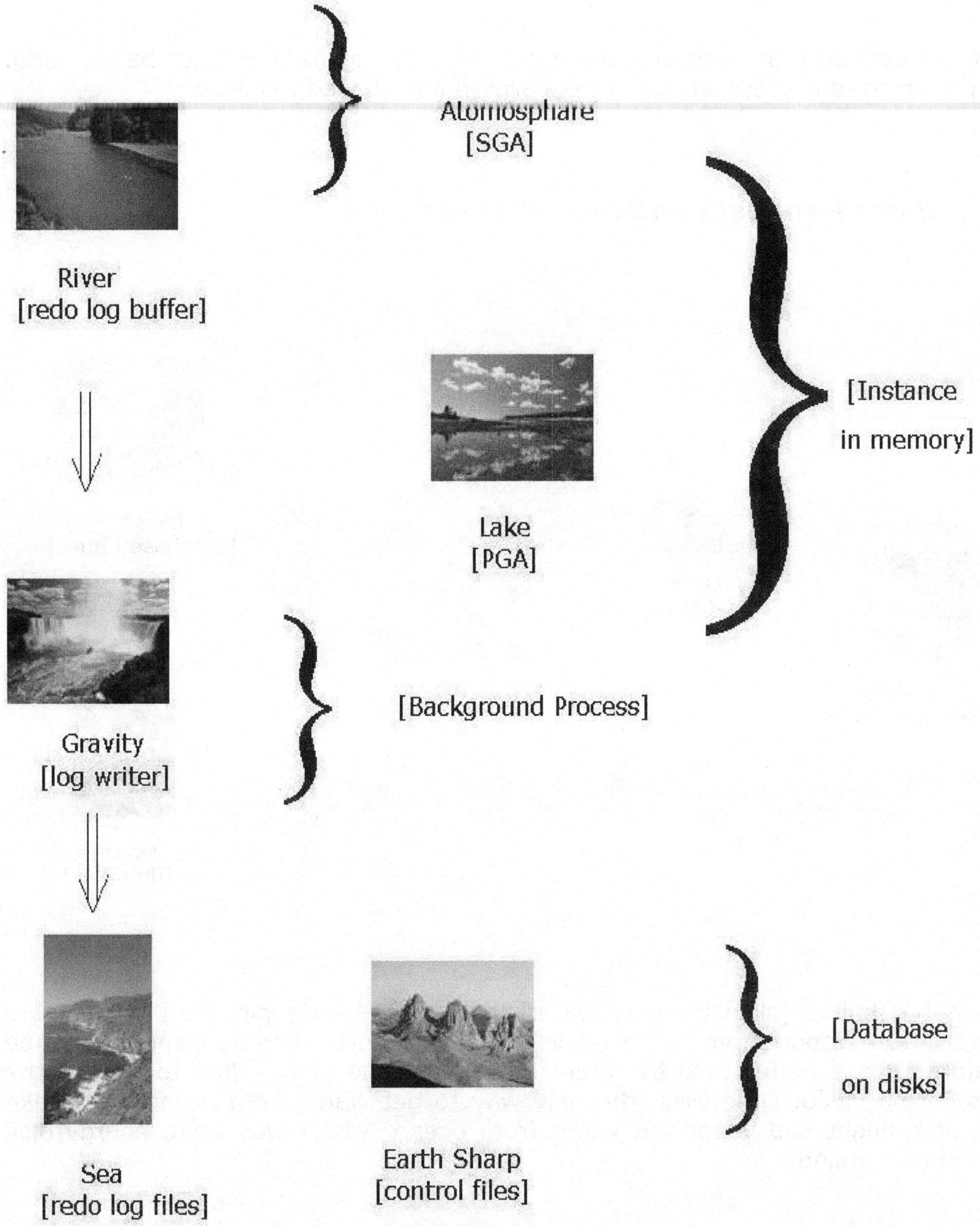
Atomosphare
[SGA]
River
[redo log buffer]
Lake
[PGA]
[Instance
in memory]
Gravity
[log writer]
[Background Process]
Sea
[redo log files]
Earth Sharp
[control files]
[Database
on disks]

Few yet noticed that Fogg actually had a very strong mathematics background. He preferred to express whatever he learnt in data-based manners.

### 1.1. Client Requests and Server Processes

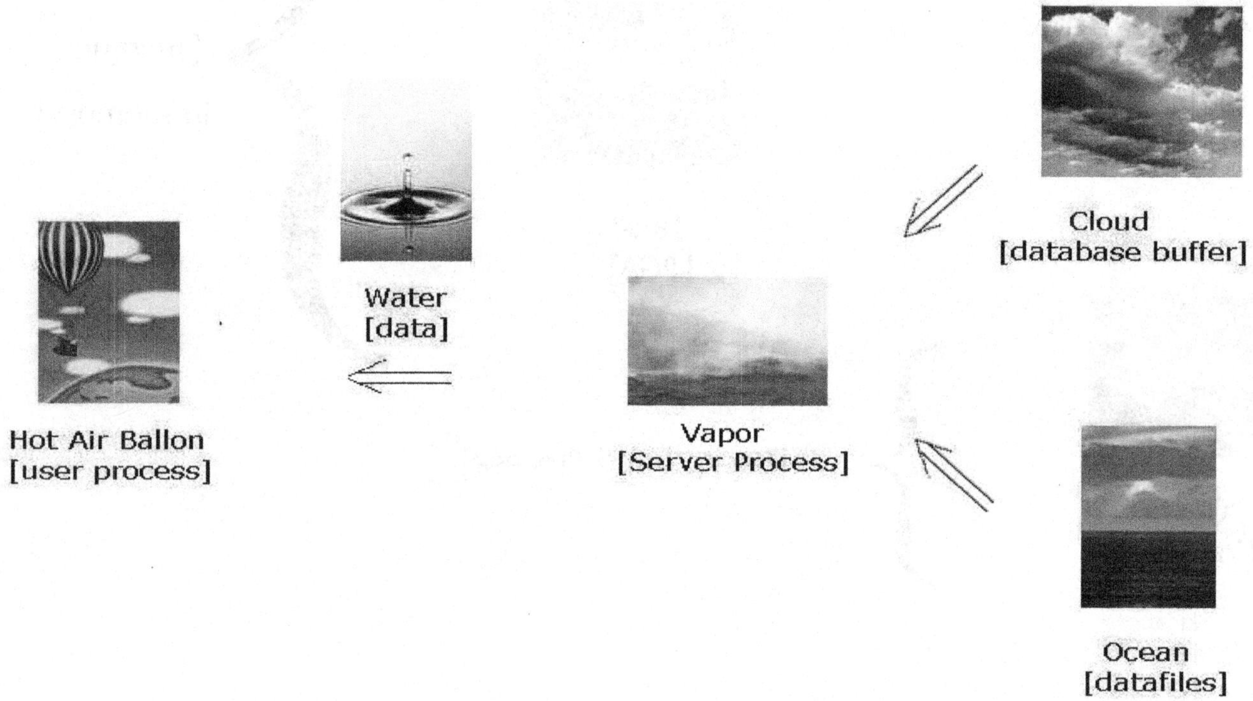


When the balloon[client]* need water[data], condensing pipe can be used to extract from vapor[server process] in the atmosphere. If there happened to be cloud[database buffer] nearby, then the job became easy - just to extract the water from cloud. Otherwise, the only way to get water from ocean was make use of sunlight and vapor the water from ocean, which was quite energy[disk wring] consuming.

* *Oracle Terminology*

## *1.2. Datafiles and Database Buffer*

Ocean[data files], as the primary source of water[data] , when heated by the Sunlight [disk read I/O], vapor the water to make up the cloud[database buffer];

On the contrary way, rain[ database writer] dropped the condensed water[dirty data] from cloud[database buffer] back to ocean[data files];

### *1.3. Redo Log File and Redo Log Buffer*

Water[redo data] flowed from river[redo log buffer] into sea[redo log file] by gravity[log writer process].

### *1.4. Database Buffer and Redo Log Buffer*

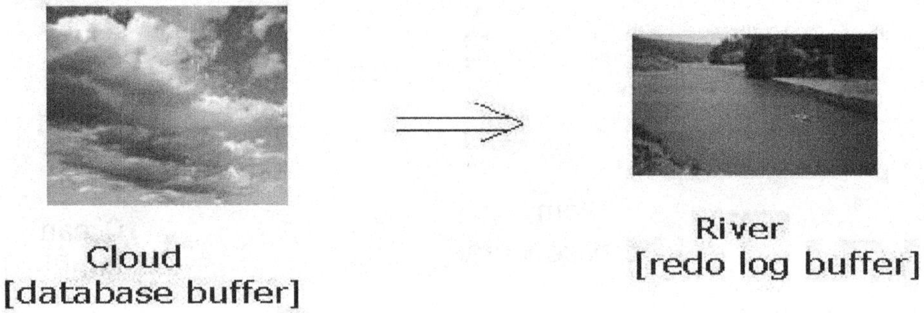


When cloud[database buffer] has grown to be too heavy, condensed water would be dropped into the river by the rain, therefore, river[redo log buffer] was reflecting the changes in cloud[database buffer].

## 1.5. Checkpoints

The trip was delayed for one day because of a heavy rain. Even so, Fogg was still very excited on the starting day because the sky was extremely clean after the rain and ideal for traveling. He marked a checkpoint on his dairy, "On the starting day, we cannot see any dirty cloud in the whole sky after the rain".

[Database writer process to flush dirty buffer to data file and checkpoint process to update data file header and control file with system change number].

## 1.6. Archive Mode versus Noarchivelog Mode

Fogg continued reading Geography on the balloon, although never set his foot out of London, Fogg had full of imagination. He was curious to know how the river intersects the sea.

He remembered how London people overcome the water shortage in the war times, when they walked long distance to fetch water with buckets from a public water pipe, "Consider sea as a bucket, river as pipe", he was imaging, "Switch the pipe from a filed bucket to another empty one [log switch]". When worked this manner, there was no wasting and all water has been archived. [The database is in archive mode.]

After the war was over and no more water shortage when Fogg passed by the same place, the pipe was still running, but no one was care about it and no bucket was available on site. Water flew away and was not archived. [Database is in the no archive mode, no log switch, log file reused. online backup cannot perform, all changes make to database since last backup will lost].

## 1.7. Database Creation

Due to his religion, Fogg believed that the world was created by the God. How did the God create the earth at first place? He was not able to find the answer in his Geography books but he imaged that the powerful supernatural made our world in the following steps:

Step One,
To write down the structure of atmosphere[SGA] on a piece of board, this board was call "init.ora";

Step Two,
With the parameters written on the board[init.ora], he built up atmosphere[SGA] including air[shared pool] and cloud[database buffer]. [Instance started by startup no mount command].

Step Three,
With atmosphere setup, he created earth sharp [create control file, contains data/log files names and locations, log sequence number and checkpoint information]. The earth sharp[control files] decided the characteristic of ocean[data files] and sea[log files].

Step Four,
With earth sharp built, he put the ocean[data files] and sea[log files] in place [Mount database], and then added/dropped/renamed ocean[data files] and sea[redo log files] at this stage.

Step five,
With all above ready, he opened the earth to all lives[open database], which means any living creatures [users with the create session privilege] could live on the earth[login to the database].

Fogg's balloon journey was quite smooth all the time until one of the most insurmountable barrier - Himalaya Mountains came into their way. When landed, they found themselves arrive in the wonderful land – India.

*Phileas Fogg and his companions, mingling in the rear ranks of the crowd, followed; and in two minutes they reached the banks of the stream, and stopped fifty paces from the pyre, upon which still lay the rajah's corpse. In the semi-obscurity they saw the victim, quite senseless, stretched out beside her husband's body. Then a torch was brought, and the wood, heavily soaked with oil, instantly took fire.*

*At this moment Sir Francis and the guide seized Phileas Fogg, who, in an instant of mad generosity, was about to rush upon the pyre. But the whole scene suddenly changed. A cry of terror arose. The whole multitude prostrated themselves, terror-stricken, on the ground.*

*The old rajah was not dead, then, since he rose of a sudden, like a spectre, took up his wife in his arms, and descended from the pyre in the midst of the clouds of smoke, which only heightened his ghostly appearance.*

*Fakirs and soldiers and priests, seized with instant terror, lay there, with their faces on the ground, not daring to lift their eyes and behold such a prodigy.*

*The resuscitated rajah approached Sir Francis and Mr. Fogg, and, in an abrupt tone, said, "Let us be off!"*

*It was Passepartout himself, who had slipped upon the pyre in the midst of the smoke and, profiting by the still overhanging darkness, had delivered the young woman from death!*

*A moment after all four of the party had disappeared in the woods, and the elephant was bearing them away at a rapid pace. But the cries and noise, and a ball which whizzed through Phileas Fogg's hat, apprised them that the trick had been discovered. Fortunately, the latter rapidly increased the distance between them, and ere long found themselves beyond the reach of the bullets and arrows.*

*– From Jules Verne, <<Around the World in 80 Days>>*

# Chapter Two Oracle Network Configuration

When Fogg and his companions passed by a splendid temple after the rash exploit, Aouda, with a wish to pay back to the God who saved her life, suggested a visit to the temple.

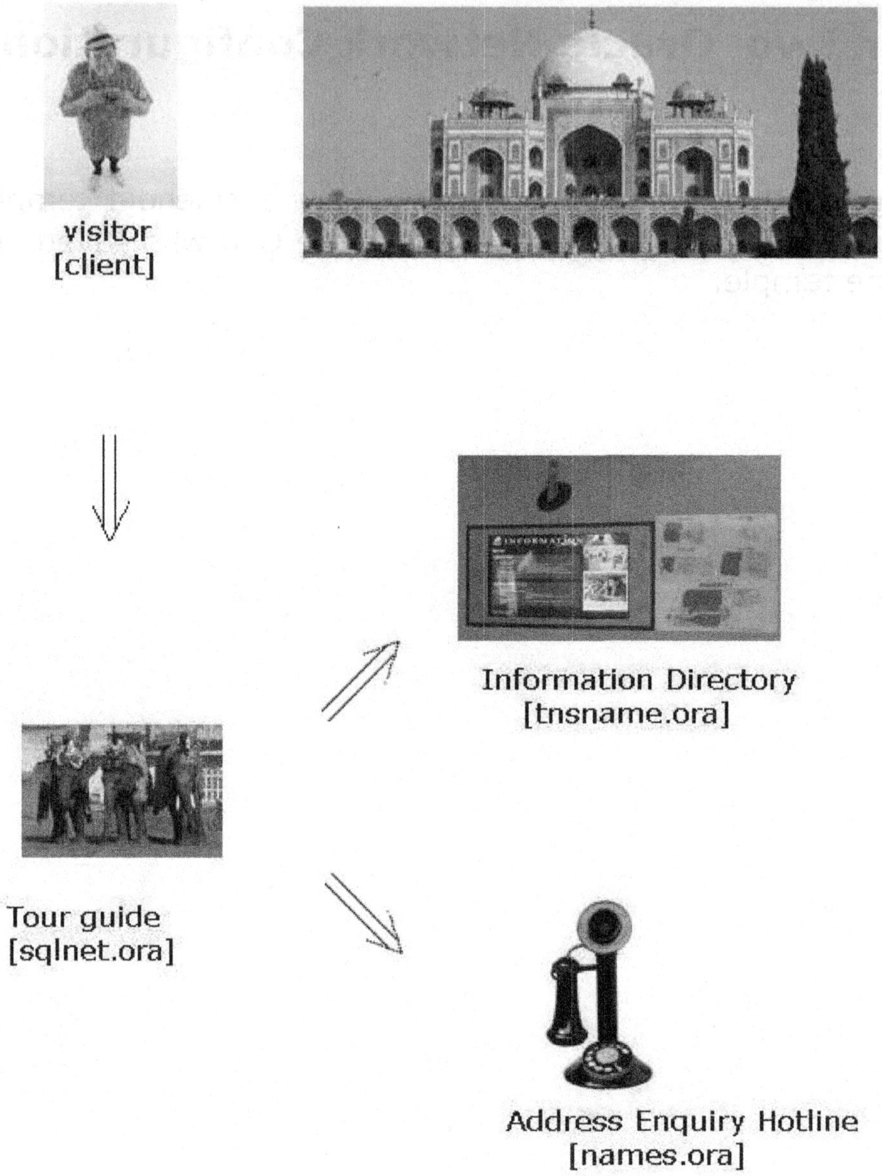
visitor
[client]
Information Directory
[tnsname.ora]
Tour guide
[sqlnet.ora]
Address Enquiry Hotline
[names.ora]

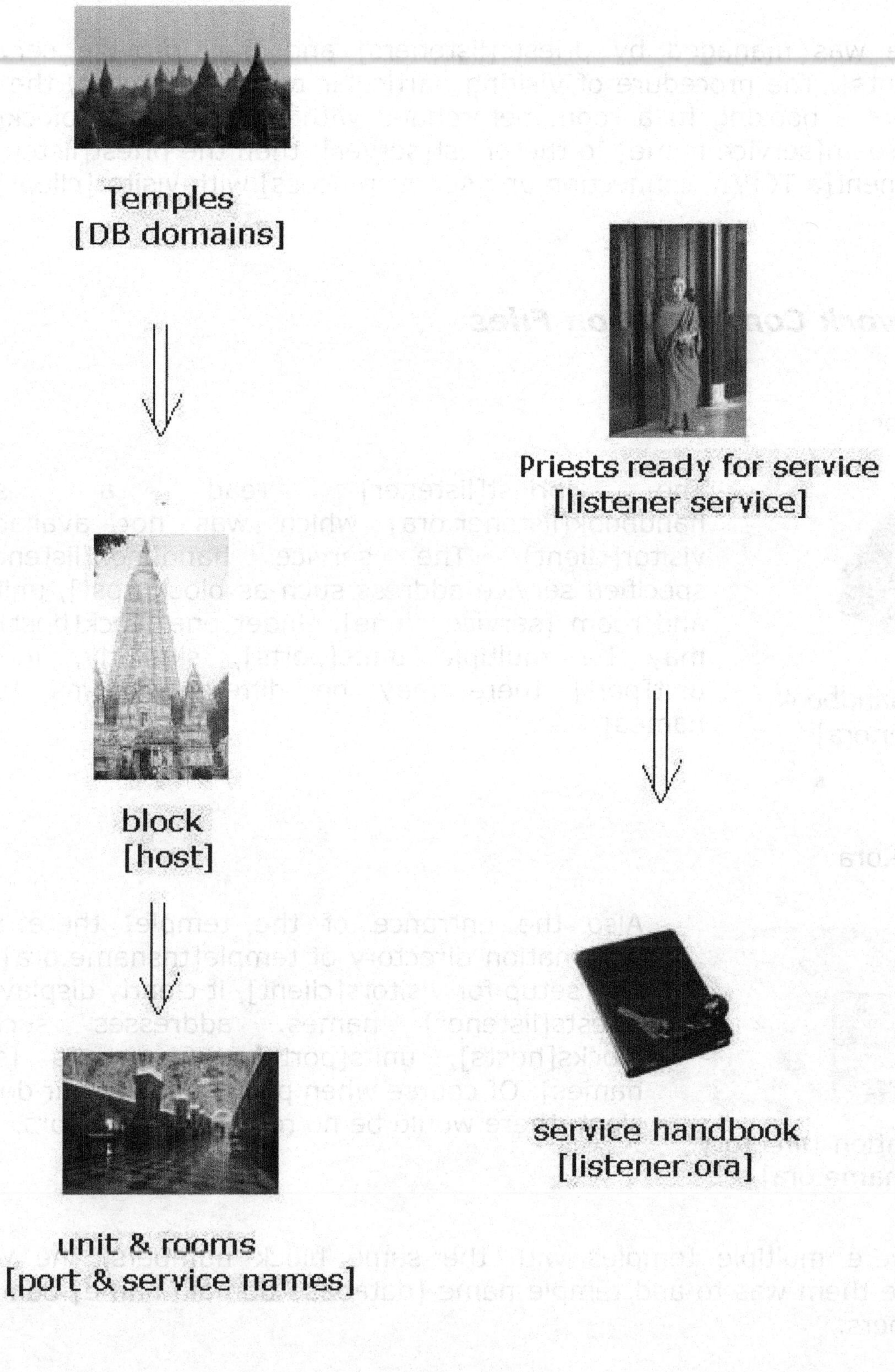
Temples
[DB domains]
Priests ready for service
[listener service]
block
[host]
service handbook
[listener.ora]
unit & rooms
[port & service names]

## 2.1. Client Request and Listener

The temple was managed by priests[listeners] and they provide service to visitors[clients]. The procedure of visiting particular temple rule was, the visitor had to make a booking to a room beforehand with full details of block[host], unit[port], room[service name] to the priest[server], then the priest[listener] set an appointment[a TCP/IP connection and server process] with visitor[client].

## 2.2. Network Configuration Files

A. listener.ora

service handbook
[listener.ora]

The priest[listener] read a service handbook[listener.ora] which was not available to visitor[client]. The service handbook[listener.ora] specified service address such as block[host], unit[port] and room [service name]. Under one block[host] there may be multiple units[ports], similarly, in same unit[port] there may be different rooms [service names].

B. tnsname.ora

Information Directory
[tnsname.ora]

Also the entrance of the temple, there was a information directory of temple[tnsname.ora] which was setup for visitors[client], it clearly displayed the priests[listener] names, addresses such as blocks[hosts], units[ports] and rooms [service names]. Of course when priest closed their door and slept, there would be no response to visitors.

If there were multiple temples with the same block numbers, the way to differentiate them was to add temple name [database domain name] behind the block numbers.

C. sqlnet.ora and names.ora

The whole trip was directed by the tour guide [sqlnet.ora]. Instead of guiding Fogg to read from the information directory of temple[tnsname.ora], he had a brand new idea.

Tour guide
[sqlnet.ora]

Address Enquiry Hotline
[names.ora]

As the modern technology started to be introduced in the temple, an address lookup hotline[names.ora] has been setup in order to improve the temple services, In that address lookup hotline[names.ora], name details of many priests[listeners] was recorded.

The tour guide [sqlnet.ora] wrote down the address lookup hotline number[names server address] and guided Fogg to use it with more conveience.

## *2.3. Listener Static and Dynamic Register*

When the priest[listener] started working[listener start], it could get instruction from service handbook[listener.ora] and then started its service [ static service registration].

However one day a priest found the service book was not latest updated, instead of reading service handbook[listener.ora], he checked the room availability information on site [get instance name, or database name from init.ora ] and then started the service [ dynamic service registration].

## *2.4. Listener Failover and Load Balance*

Further improvement was that the priests were separated into 3 shifts to cover 24 hours, if one group slept, another group took over [listener failover] .

Also within the same shift, more than one priests working at a time, each received same number of visitors[clients]. [listener load balance].

When all came out of the temple, Sir Francis told Phileas Fogg that he noticed someone suspicious in the temple and should Aouda remain in India, she would inevitably fall again into the hands of her executioners. Therefore she would only be safe by quitting India for ever.

*Fix had no time to lose: Fogg must be detained at Hong Kong, the last foothold of English territory. so he resolved to make a clean breast of it.*

*"Listen to me," said Fix abruptly. "I am not, as you think, an agent of the members of the Reform Club--, I am a police detective, sent out here by the London office."*

*"You, a detective?"*

*"I will prove it. Here is my commission."*

*Passepartout was speechless with astonishment when Fix displayed this document, the genuineness of which could not be doubted.*

*"Listen. On the 28th of last September a robbery of fifty-five thousand pounds was committed at the Bank of England by a person whose description was fortunately secured. Here is his description; it answers exactly to that of Mr. Phileas Fogg."*

*"What nonsense!" cried Passepartout, striking the table with his fist. "My master is the most honourable of men!"*

*"I will share with you the two thousand pounds reward offered by the Bank of England."*

*"Mr. Fix," he stammered, "even should what you say be true-- if my master is really the robber you are seeking for--which I deny-- I have been, am, in his service; I have seen his generosity and goodness; and I will never betray him--not for all the gold in the world. I come from a village where they don't eat that kind of bread!"*

*"You refuse?"*

*"I refuse."*

*"Consider that I've said nothing," said Fix; "and let us drink."*

*"Yes; let us drink!"*

*Passepartout felt himself yielding more and more to the effects of the liquor. Fix, seeing that he must, at all hazards, be separated from his master, wished to entirely overcome him.*

*"At last!" said Fix, seeing Passepartout unconscious.*

*"Mr. Fogg will not be informed of the Carnatic's departure; and, if he is, he will have to go without this cursed Frenchman!"*

*and, after paying his bill, Fix left the tavern.*

*– From Jules Verne, <<Around the World in 80 Days>>*

## Chapter Three  Database Grid Control

Fix was accompanied Fogg all the time during his trip without his identity as a detective been discovered. Waiting for the warrant of arrest from London which was only valid in the English colony territory, he wanted to know more about the British colony.

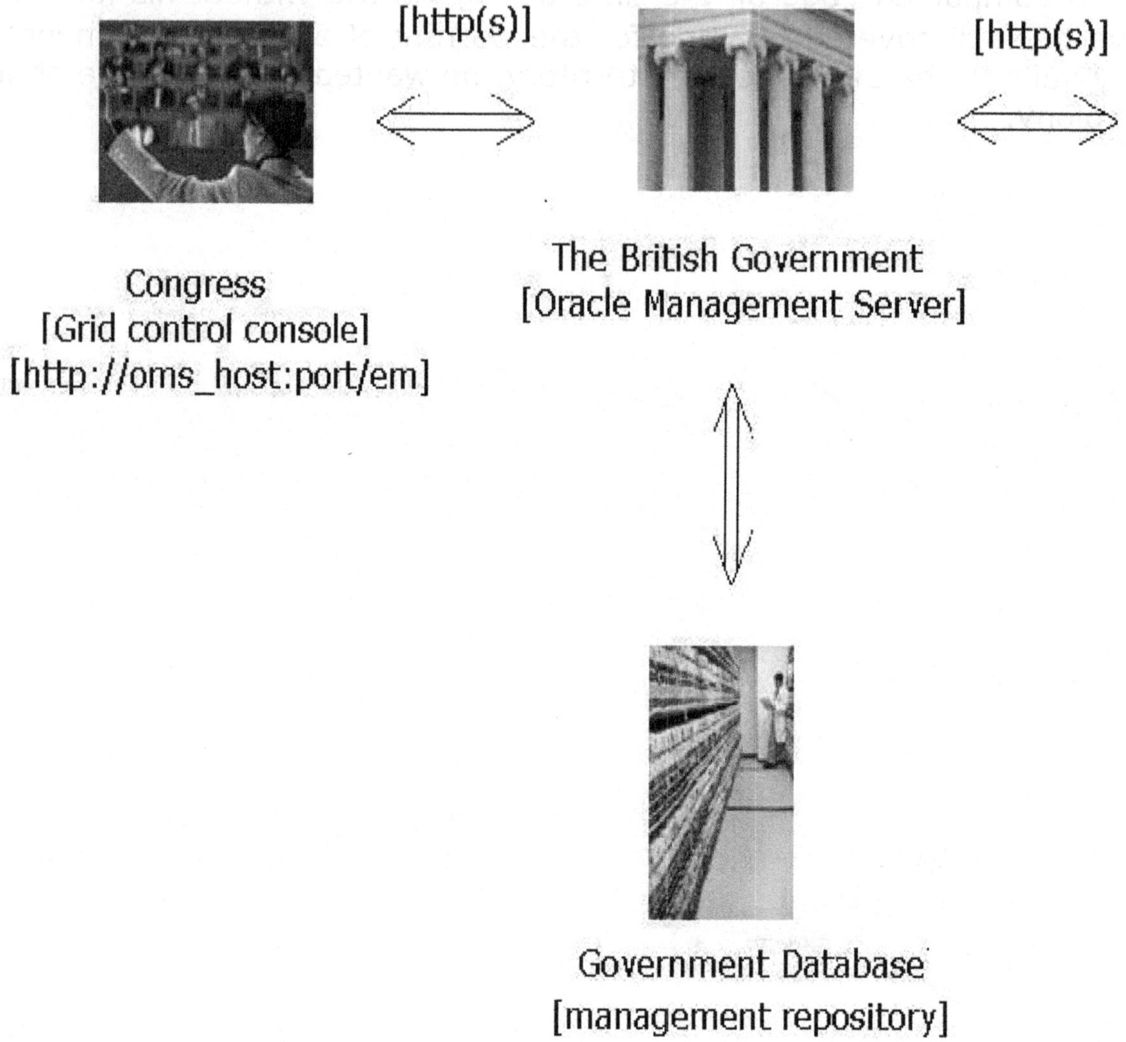
[http(s)]
[http(s)]
Congress
[Grid control console]
[http://oms_host:port/em]
The British Government
[Oracle Management Server]
Government Database
[management repository]

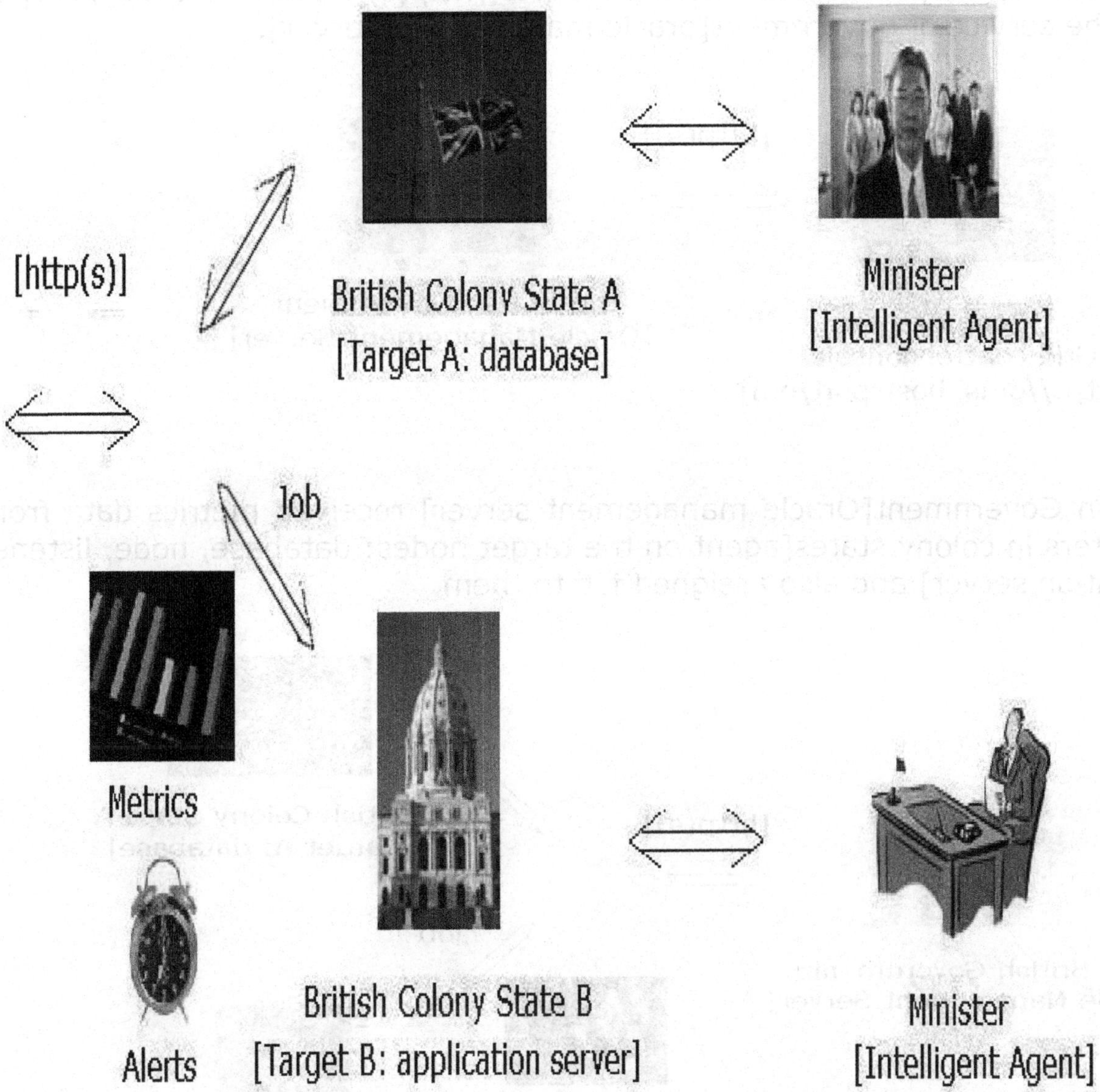
[http(s)]
British Colony State A
[Target A: database]
Minister
[Intelligent Agent]
Job
Metrics
Alerts
British Colony State B
[Target B: application server]
Minister
[Intelligent Agent]

### *3.1. Grid Control Structure*

The Congress[grid control console], as the head of British government[Oracle management server], used the internal reports [http(s)://oms_host:port/em] to monitor the service of government[oracle management server].

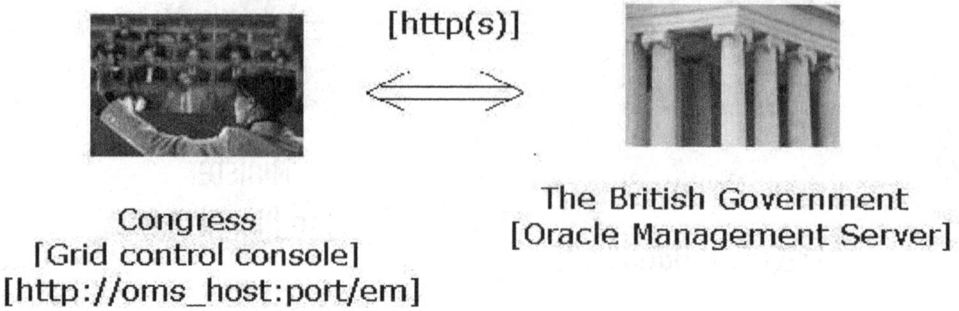


The British Government[Oracle management server] received metrics data from the ministers in colony states[agent on the target nodes: database, node, listener or application server] and also assigned job to them.

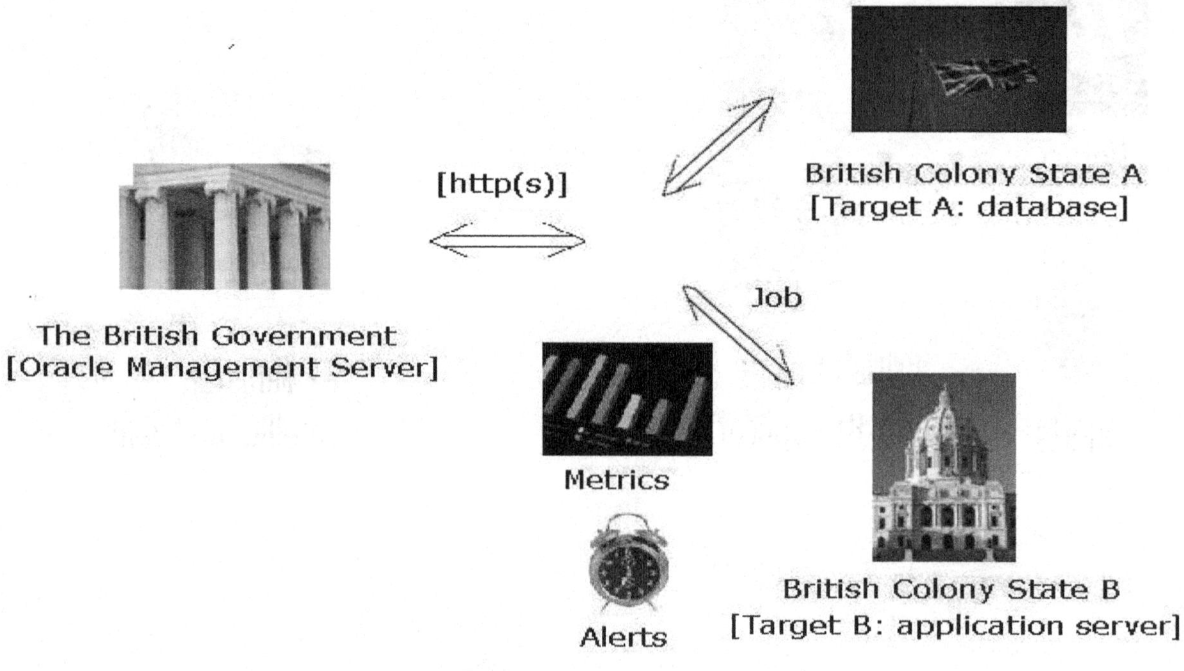

The Government[Oracle management server] also setup a government database[management repository owned by sysman] to collect and store colony[agent on the target node] information

Government Database
[management repository]

### 3.2. Metrics and Alerts

In order to monitor efficiently, the Congress[grid control console] has setup a metrics(units of measurement), with thresholds such as unemployment rate, criminal rate, etc. associated, to assess the management status of each colony state[target node].

The Government[Oracle management server] had to check the metrics at a certain intervals, if the thresholds had been reached, or the availability of services changes, alert would be generated.

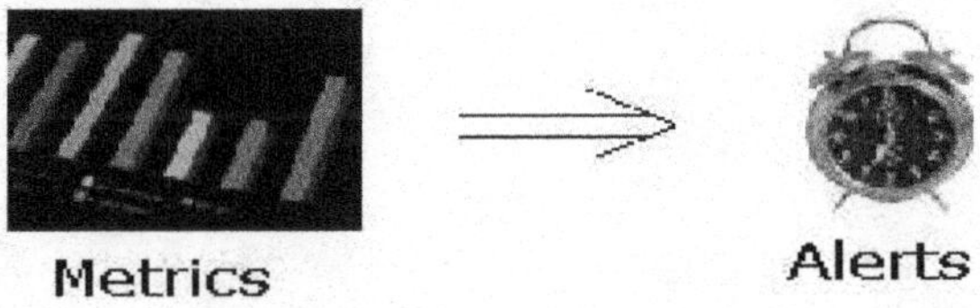


In case of alert, the government[oracle management server] would be notified by mail [email/paging/SNMP traps/custom scripts]. The type of alerts can be classified by problem[such as database down], bad performance[performance/resource threshold reach] or others[ user defined test].

### 3.3. Scheduled Job

The Government[Oracle management server] assigned jobs to minister on colony states[agent on the target node] to execute certain tasks [such as the database up down] and sent back the results to the government [oracle management server].

The job, normally a maintenance type[analyze, import/export, backup/recovery, run SQL script, shutdown/startup database] would be finally executed by ministers on colony states[agent on the target nodes].

The next morning when Passepartout found himself on the deck of the Carnatic leaving for Japan without his master on board, he fell thunderstruck on a seat.

*Passepartout went upon the stage, and took his place beside the rest who were to compose the base of the Car of Juggernaut. They all stretched themselves on the floor, their noses pointing to the ceiling. A second group of artists disposed themselves on these long appendages, then a third above these, then a fourth, until a human monument reaching to the very cornices of the theatre soon arose on top of the noses. This elicited loud applause, in the midst of which the orchestra was just striking up a deafening air, when the pyramid tottered, the balance was lost, one of the lower noses vanished from the pyramid, and the human monument was shattered like a castle built of cards!*

*It was Passepartout's fault. Abandoning his position, clearing the footlights without the aid of his wings, and, clambering up to the right-hand gallery, he fell at the feet of one of the spectators, crying, "Ah, my master! my master!"*

*"You here?"*

*"Myself."*

*"Very well; then let us go to the steamer, young man!"*

*Mr. Fogg, Aouda, and Passepartout passed through the lobby of the theatre to the outside, where they encountered the Honourable Mr. Batulcar, furious with rage. He demanded damages for the "breakage" of the pyramid; and Phileas Fogg appeased him by giving him a handful of banknotes.*

*At half-past six, the very hour of departure, Mr. Fogg and Aouda, followed by Passepartout, who in his hurry had retained his wings, and nose six feet long, stepped upon the American steamer.*

*– From Jules Verne, <<Around the World in 80 Days>>*

# Chapter Four  Backup, Recovery and RMAN

Fogg was a fan of acrobatics. Upon arriving Japan the first thing he did was to watch a long nose acrobatic show.

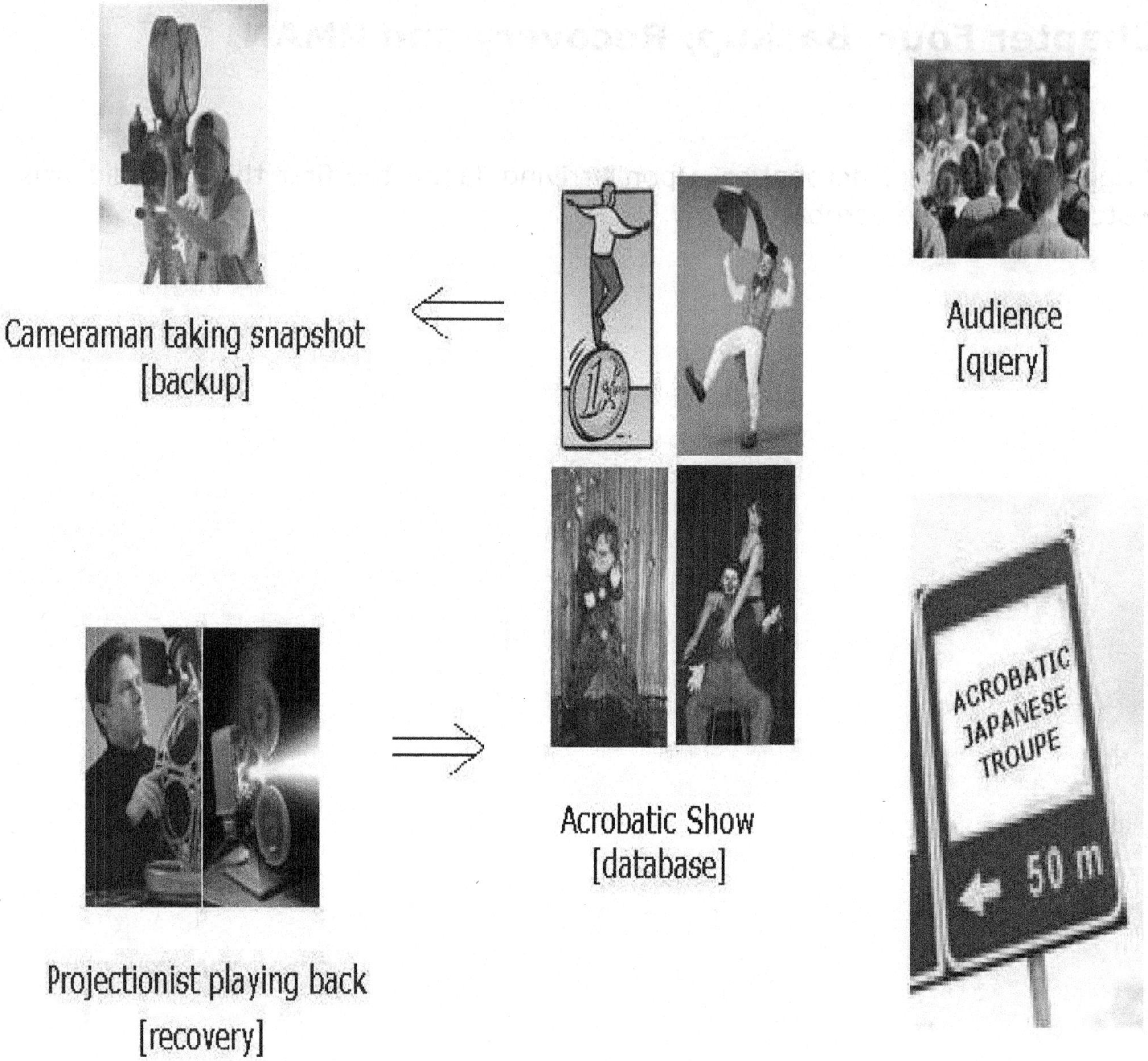
Cameraman taking snapshot
[backup]
Audience
[query]
ACROBATIC
JAPANESE
TROUPE
50 m
Projectionist playing back
[recovery]
Acrobatic Show
[database]

Show Program Menu
[redo log buffer]
Show Act Sequence Number
[System Change Number, SCN]

Show Director
[control file]

Discrete Film
[datafile]

+

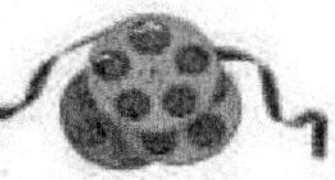

Progressive Film
[redo log file]

Film Catalogue
[recovery catalogue]

Media Company
[rman utility]

## *4.1. System Change Number(SCN)*

When he reached the cabin, Fogg noticed the director[control file] writing the act title of each program with an act sequence number[SCN] on a show program menu[redo log buffer], What this act sequence number [SCN] used for?

Reason One : For Database Consistent

Show Director
[control file]

The director[control file] kept track of the show by an act sequence number[SCN]. In the mean time, the acrobats[data files] of the troupe also kept an act sequence number[SCN] for their own synchronization purpose.

Show Program Menu
[redo log buffer]
Show Act Sequence Number
[System Change Number, SCN]

The coordinator[SMON] played an important role in the troupe. At beginning of the show[database], he checked these two sequence number[SCN] of both director and acrobats, if matches, then only he started the show [database]. Otherwise, he would take some actions[recovery steps] to avoid the show[database] to be performed in an inconsistent state.

When the director was moving faster:
(The act sequence number[SCN] of director [control file] was higher than that of the acrobats has played)

In order to synchronize the show, the coordinator[SMON] asked the acrobats[data file] continued to play until reach the act sequence number[SCN] of director [control file].
[To apply archive redo logs to data files, either incompletely (to a certain point of time/SCN/log sequence#) or completely(to most recent SCN)].

When the acrobats was moving faster:
(The act sequence number[SCN] of acrobats[data file] was higher than what direct has noticed)

In order to synchronize the show, the coordinator[SMON] asked the acrobats[data file] to replay[recover] from the beginning.
[To issue recover command including "using backup control file"].

Reason Two : For Query Consistent

Fogg experienced unhappy experience with the show, due to the poor arrangement of the theater.

When the audience started watching the show [a query start reads a data block], the audience[query] get the ticket for the show program[block SCN] at the Theater A.

However, the show program[block SCN] was changed at last minutes after the show started. Audiences[query] had to find the same program[block SCN] from a standby area[rollback segments] called Theater B, but even worse was that, Theater B was under maintenance and not available as well!

Everyone cannot stop the angry and complain["snapshot too old" error] came out.

### *4.2. Online Backup*

Cameraman taking snapshot
[backup]

⟸

Acrobatic Show
[database]

When the photographer taking snapshot[backup], act sequence number[SCN] of all acrobats[data files] must be the same.

To achieve this, the coordinator initiate a checkpoint to the acrobats[data file] so that all the acrobats[data files] has same act sequence number[SCN] before snapshot[backup] was taken .

[alter tablespace begin/end backup -database must in archivelog mode, check the tablespace status from v$backup, that is, if v$backup still show active, tablespace and datafile is still in backup mode]

### *4.3. Recovery*

At that time, film capacity was not large enough to keep recording for too long, therefore, photographers had to use two films: a discrete film[datafile] and progressive films[redo log files]. The discrete film was used to take snapshots every 5 seconds, while the progressive film[redo] to record only the changes but continuously.

Discrete Film
[datafile]

+

Progressive Film
[redo log file]

Complete Recovery:

Projectionist played back to a certain point of historic time use discrete film[datafile] only.
[steps:
1. Restore all database files
2. startup mount;
3. recover database;
(apply archive redo log files)
4. alter database open;]

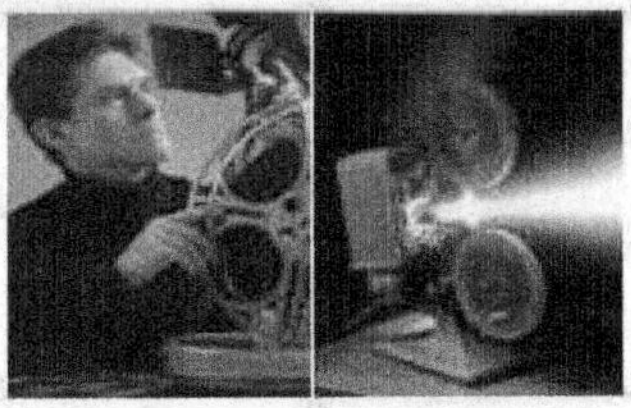

Projectionist playing back
[recovery]

Acrobatic Show
[database]

Incomplete Recovery:

Projectionist played back to a certain point of historic time use both the discrete film[datafile] and the progressive films[redo log files]
[steps:
1. Restore all database files except redo log files
2 startup mount;
3 recover database until cancel/time/change
(Apply archive redo log files until a certain point)
4. alter database open resetlogs;]

### *4.4. Oracle Recovery Manager(RMAN)*

Film Catalogue
[recovery catalogue]

Media Company
[rman utility]

Due to the market competition, the job of cameraman and projectionist were taken over by a media company [rman utility], due to the advantage that the company not only provided photographing and playing back [backup and recovery] service, but also provided film catalogue[recovery catalogue] maintenance service as following:

A. To query film catalogue[recovery catalogue]
The film catalogue[recovery catalogue] can be visited.
[rman commands: list/report]

B. To maintain film catalogue[recovery catalogue]: resynchronization

When the show changed its title or show time, company's film catalogue[recovery catalogue] needed to be updated.
[recovery catalog and database control file can be synchronized with crosscheck command]

At half-past six, the very hour of departure, Mr. Fogg and Aouda, followed by Passepartout, who in his hurry had retained his wings, and nose six feet long, stepped upon the American steamer.

*This was not the first attempt of these daring Indians, for more than once they had waylaid trains on the road. A hundred of them had, according to their habit, jumped upon the steps without stopping the train, with the ease of a clown mounting a horse at full gallop.*

*The Indians had first mounted the engine, and half stunned the engineer and stoker with blows from their muskets. A Sioux chief, wishing to stop the train, but not knowing how to work the regulator, had opened wide instead of closing the steam-valve, and the locomotive was plunging forward with terrific velocity.*

*The Sioux had at the same time invaded the cars, skipping like enraged monkeys over the roofs, thrusting open the doors, and fighting hand to hand with the passengers. Penetrating the baggage-car, they pillaged it, throwing the trunks out of the train. The cries and shots were constant. The travellers defended themselves bravely; some of the cars were barricaded, and sustained a siege, like moving forts, carried along at a speed of a hundred miles an hour.*

*It was necessary to put an end to the struggle, which had lasted for ten minutes, and which would result in the triumph of the Sioux if the train was not stopped. Fort Kearney station, where there was a garrison, was only two miles distant; but, that once passed, the Sioux would be masters of the train between Fort Kearney and the station beyond.*

*The conductor was fighting beside Mr. Fogg, when he was shot and fell. At the same moment he cried, "Unless the train is stopped in five minutes, we are lost!"*

*"It shall be stopped," said Phileas Fogg, preparing to rush from the car.*

*"Stay, monsieur," cried Passepartout; "I will go."*

*Mr. Fogg had not time to stop the brave fellow, who, opening a door unperceived by the Indians, succeeded in slipping under the car; and while the struggle continued and the balls whizzed across each other over his head, he made use of his old acrobatic experience, and with amazing agility worked his way under the cars, holding on to the chains, aiding himself by the brakes and edges of the sashes, creeping from one car to another with marvellous skill, and thus gaining the forward end of the train.*

*There, suspended by one hand between the baggage-car and the tender, with the other he loosened the safety chains; but, owing to the traction, he would never have succeeded in unscrewing the yoking-bar, had not a violent concussion jolted this bar out. The train, now detached from the engine, remained a little behind, whilst the locomotive rushed forward with increased speed.*

*Carried on by the force already acquired, the train still moved for several minutes; but the brakes were worked and at last they stopped, less than a hundred feet from Kearney station.*

*The soldiers of the fort, attracted by the shots, hurried up; the Sioux had not expected them, and decamped in a body before the train entirely stopped.*

*– From Jules Verne, <<Around the World in 80 Days>>*

## Chapter Five  Oracle Real Application Cluster(RAC)

Before starting rescue of Passepartout, Fogg was studying a railway map on a wall in the Fort Kearney station.

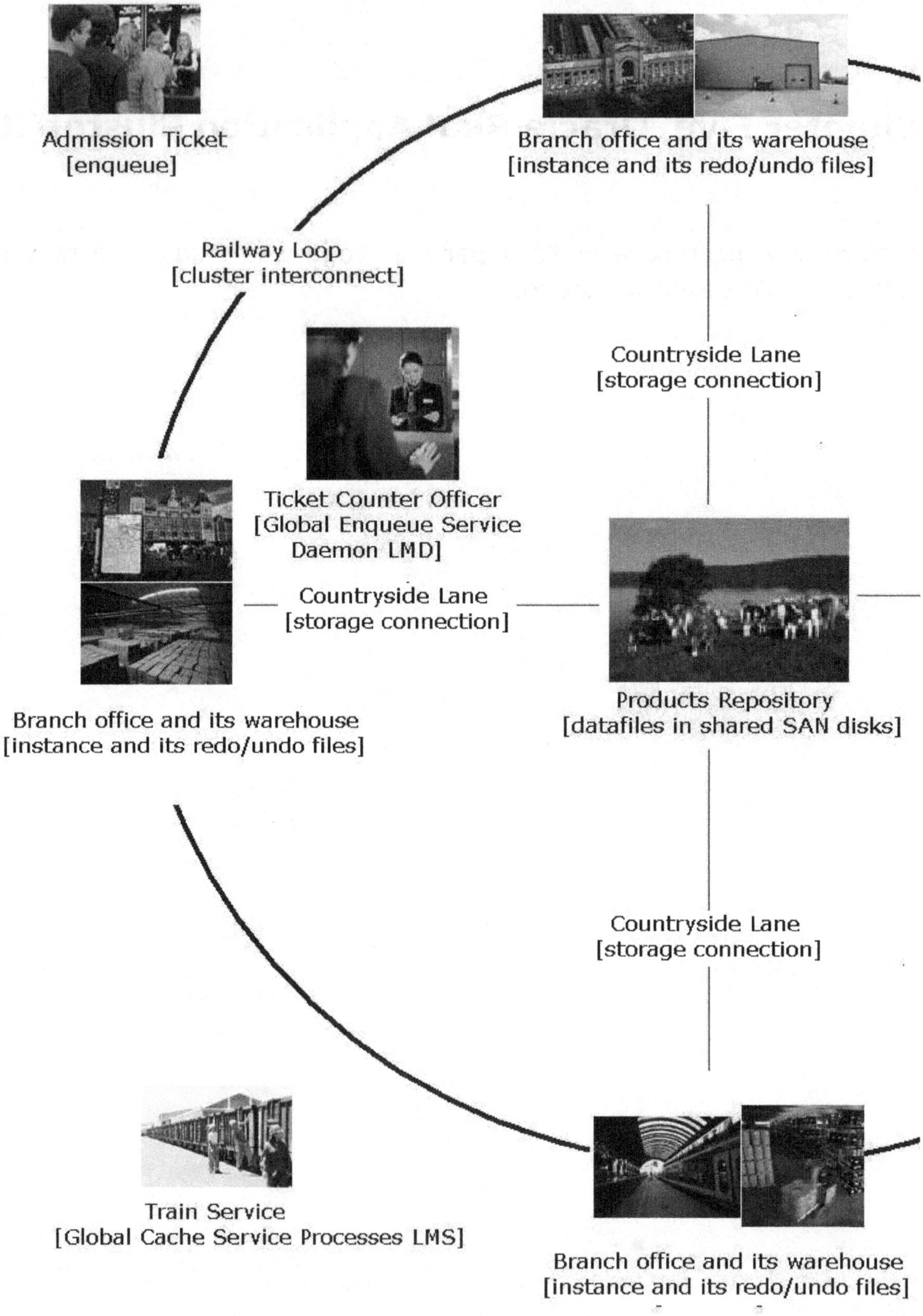

Admission Ticket
[enqueue]
Branch office and its warehouse
[instance and its redo/undo files]
Railway Loop
[cluster interconnect]
Countryside Lane
[storage connection]
Ticket Counter Officer
[Global Enqueue Service
Daemon LMD]
Countryside Lane
[storage connection]
Branch office and its warehouse
[instance and its redo/undo files]
Products Repository
[datafiles in shared SAN disks]
Countryside Lane
[storage connection]
Train Service
[Global Cache Service Processes LMS]
Branch office and its warehouse
[instance and its redo/undo files]

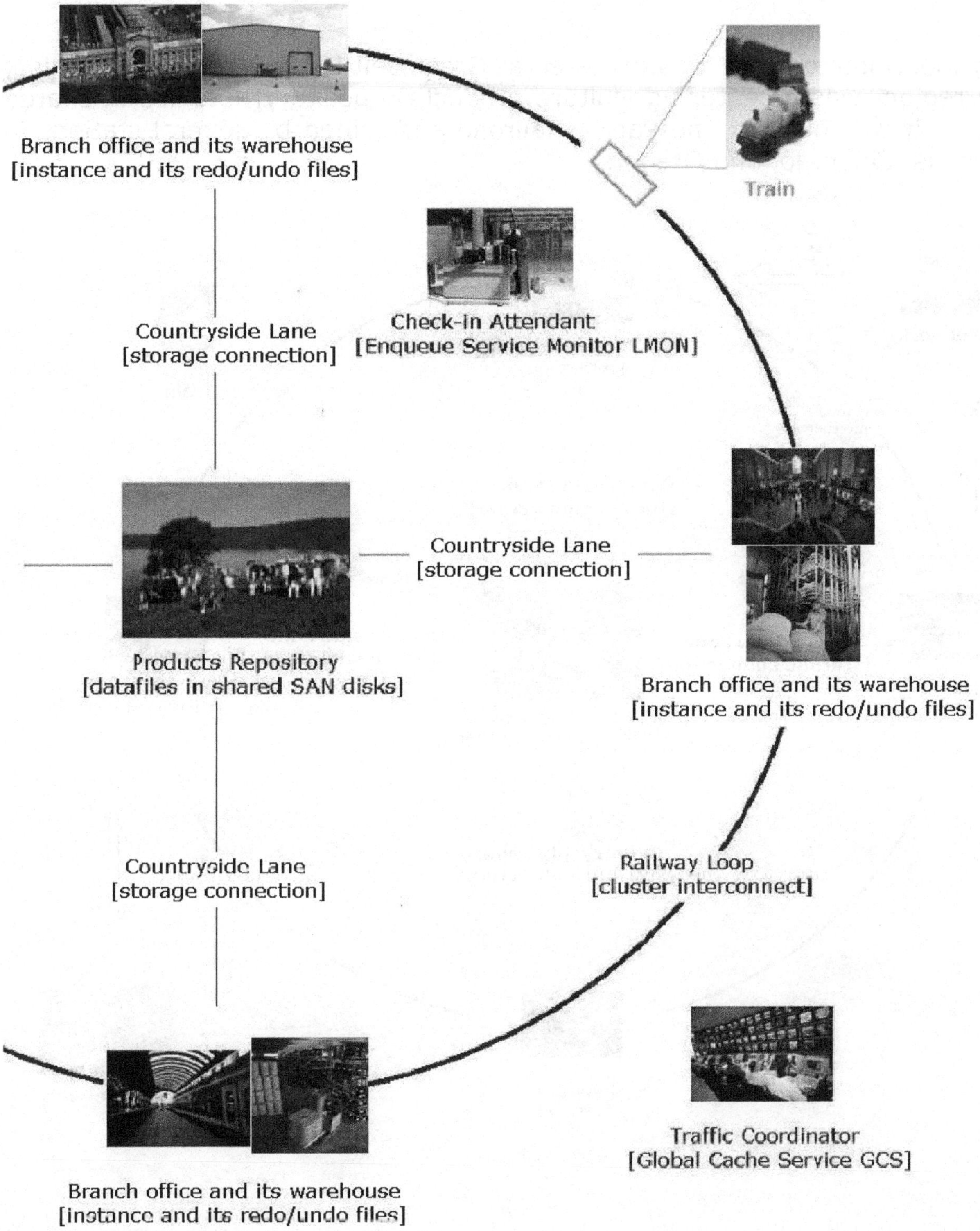
Branch office and its warehouse
[instance and its redo/undo files]
Train
Check-in Attendant
[Enqueue Service Monitor LMON]
Countryside Lane
[storage connection]
Countryside Lane
[storage connection]
Products Repository
[datafiles in shared SAN disks]
Branch office and its warehouse
[instance and its redo/undo files]
Countryside Lane
[storage connection]
Railway Loop
[cluster interconnect]
Branch office and its warehouse
[instance and its redo/undo files]
Traffic Coordinator
[Global Cache Service GCS]

## 5.1. Physical Structure

A railway loop[interconnect] was centered at Great Salt Lake, where, in the midst of fertile region, was a center agriculture products repository[datafiles in shared SAN disks]. It was built by The Pacific Railroad and joined by several stations in Iowa, Kansas, Colorado, and Oregon.

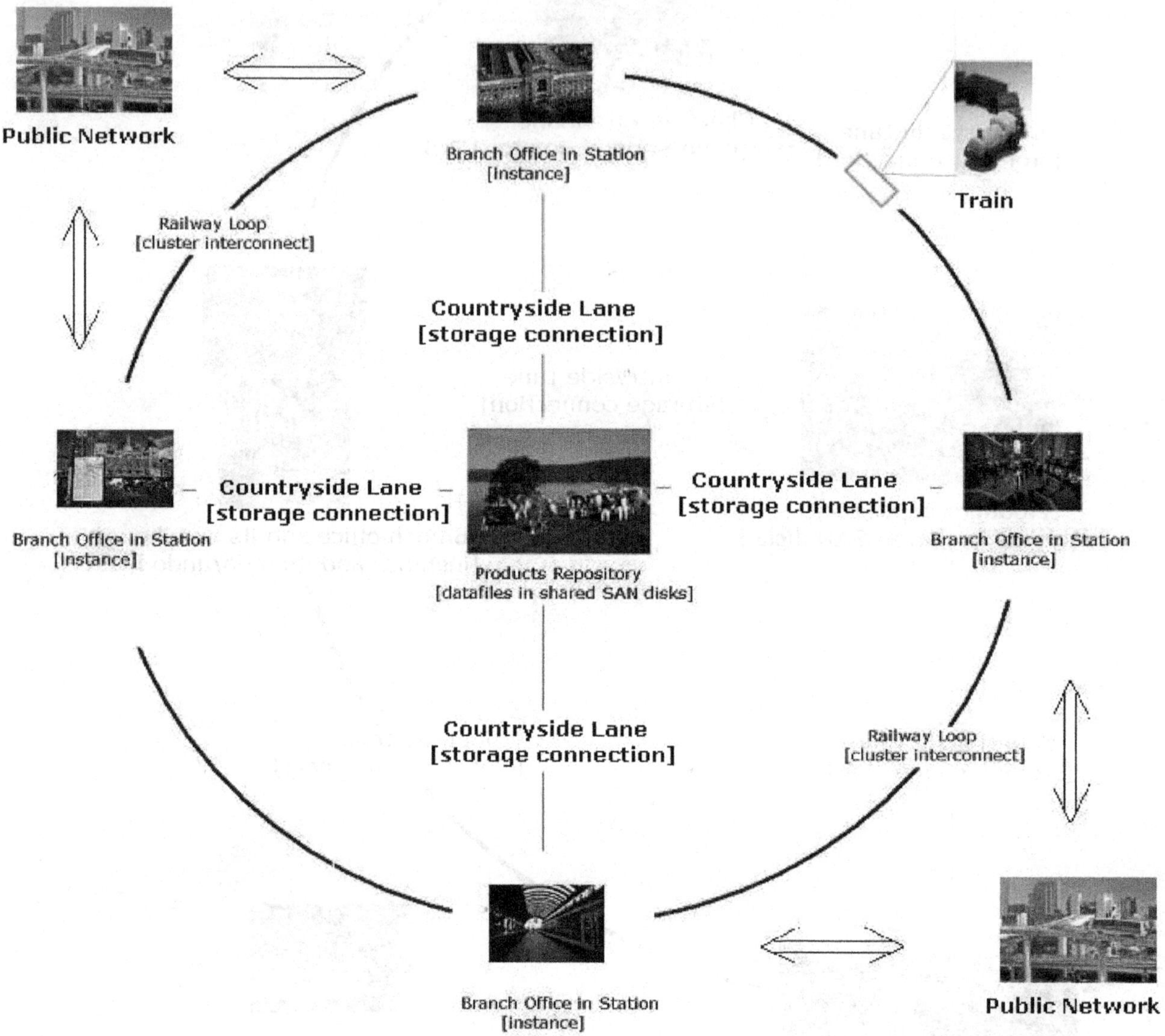

The farmers also setup multiple branch offices[instances] on each station. The advantage was that the branch office[instance] at each station equally easy to access the repository, and the products can be exchanged among the branch offices[instances].

Customers can get products directly from branch office[instance] and the branch office[instance] will finally get from its seedbed - products repository[datafiles in shared SAN disks] .

The branch offices[instance] has their own warehouses[redo and undo files] and were linked by a railway loop[cluster interconnect] for the communication and exchange products[data].

Branch office and its warehouse
[instance and its redo/undo files]

## *5.2. Resource Coordination*

At each station different products may come at the same time. To control the traffic flow, the station controller [global service daemon GSD] only issued one admission ticket[enqueue, shared memory structures that serialize row updates] at any point of time, farmers had to queue for the admission ticket[enqueue] in order to enter the gate in sequence.

Admission Ticket
[enqueue]

The usage of the ticket was controlled by those important officers:

A. Station Controller [Global Service Daemon GSD]

His job was to execute orders from manager. [To coordinates with the cluster manager to receive requests from clients such as the DBCA, EM, and the SRVCTL utility to execute administrative job tasks such as instance startup or shutdown]

Station Controller
[Global Service Daemon GSD]

B. Ticket Counter Officer[ Global Enqueue Service Daemon LMD]

Ticket Counter Officer
[Global Enqueue Service
Daemon LMD]

Her job was to process admission ticket[enqueue] request [manages global enqueue and global resource access]

C. Check-In Attendant [Enqueue Service Monitor LMON]

Check-in Attendant
[Enqueue Service Monitor LMON]

His job was to monitors admission ticket [enqueue] usage.
[monitors global enqueues and resources across the cluster and performs global enqueue recovery operations]

## *5.3. Cache Fusion*

In order to understand how the traffic of the train[memory buffer] was controlled smoothly, Fogg found that the railway was managed by the service of below:

A. Railway Traffic Coordinator[The Global Cache Service GCS]

Traffic Coordinator
[Global Cache Service GCS]

They were responsible for traffic controlling and coordination.
[Coordinating the block transfers between instances].

B. Train Service [Global Cache Service Processes LMS]

Train Service
[Global Cache Service Processes LMS]

The service was to transfer products[data] between stations[instances].

One labor-costing job was to get the product from and then send them back to the repository via the countryside lanes[storage connections] as only wagons were able to pass through. To cut the cost, the heads of each station met and came out a corporation agreement[Cache Fusion].

Under this agreement[Cache Fusion], when a branch office need a product which not available in the current station branch office[current instance's memory cache], rather than getting it from the repository, the requesting station will submit a request to the railway traffic coordinator[The Global Cache Service GCS], which in turn found out the product was located in another holding station branch office[holding instance] .

Then the train service[ Global Cache Service Processes LMSn] sent the product[data] from holding station branch office[holding instance ] to requesting station branch office[requesting instance ].

On receipt of the product[data], requesting station branch office[requesting instance ] informed the railway traffic coordinator[The Global Cache Service GCS] that it was holding the product.

In such a way, products[data] were directly transferred from a branch office[ holding instance] to a requesting station and as a result, the usage of wagons in the countryside lanes [storage connections] [disk I/O] has been reduced to a minimum.

Mr. Fogg fought the Indians ten miles south of Fort Kearney and successfully rescued Passepartout and the other two passengers from the Sioux.

*In three minutes Passepartout was in Saville Row again, and staggered back into Mr. Fogg's room. He could not speak.*

*"What is the matter?" asked Mr. Fogg.*

*"My master!" gasped Passepartout--"marriage--impossible--"*

*"Impossible?"*

*"Impossible--for to-morrow."*

*"Why so?"*

*"Because to-morrow--is Sunday!"*

*"Monday," replied Mr. Fogg.*

*"No--to-day is Saturday."*

*"Saturday? Impossible!"*

*"Yes, yes, yes, yes!" cried Passepartout. "You have made a mistake of one day! We arrived twenty-four hours ahead of time; but there are only ten minutes left!"*

*Passepartout had seized his master by the collar, and was dragging him along with irresistible force.*

*Phileas Fogg, thus kidnapped, without having time to think, left his house, jumped into a cab, promised a hundred pounds to the cabman, and, having run over two dogs and overturned five carriages, reached the Reform Club.*

*The clock indicated a quarter before nine when he appeared in the great saloon.*

*Phileas Fogg had accomplished the journey round the world in eighty days!*

*Phileas Fogg had won his wager of twenty thousand pounds!*

*– From Jules Verne, <<Around the World in 80 Days>>*

## Chapter Six Performance Tuning

Fogg had accomplished the journey just on time. However, was there any way to make the whole process more efficient and faster? He looked at the weather map and came out with many ideas of improvement.

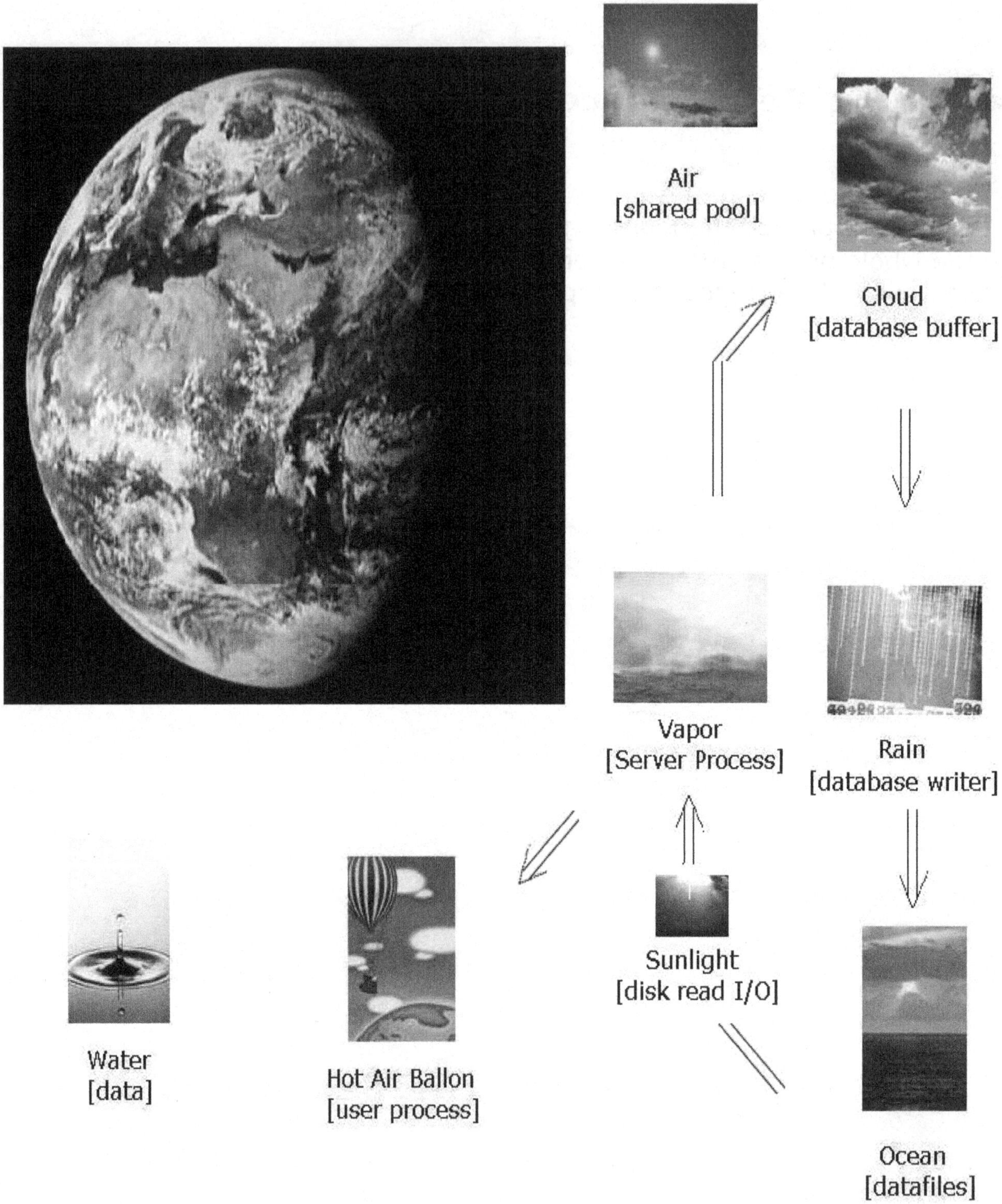
Air
[shared pool]
Cloud
[database buffer]
Vapor
[Server Process]
Rain
[database writer]
Water
[data]
Hot Air Ballon
[user process]
Sunlight
[disk read I/O]
Ocean
[datafiles]

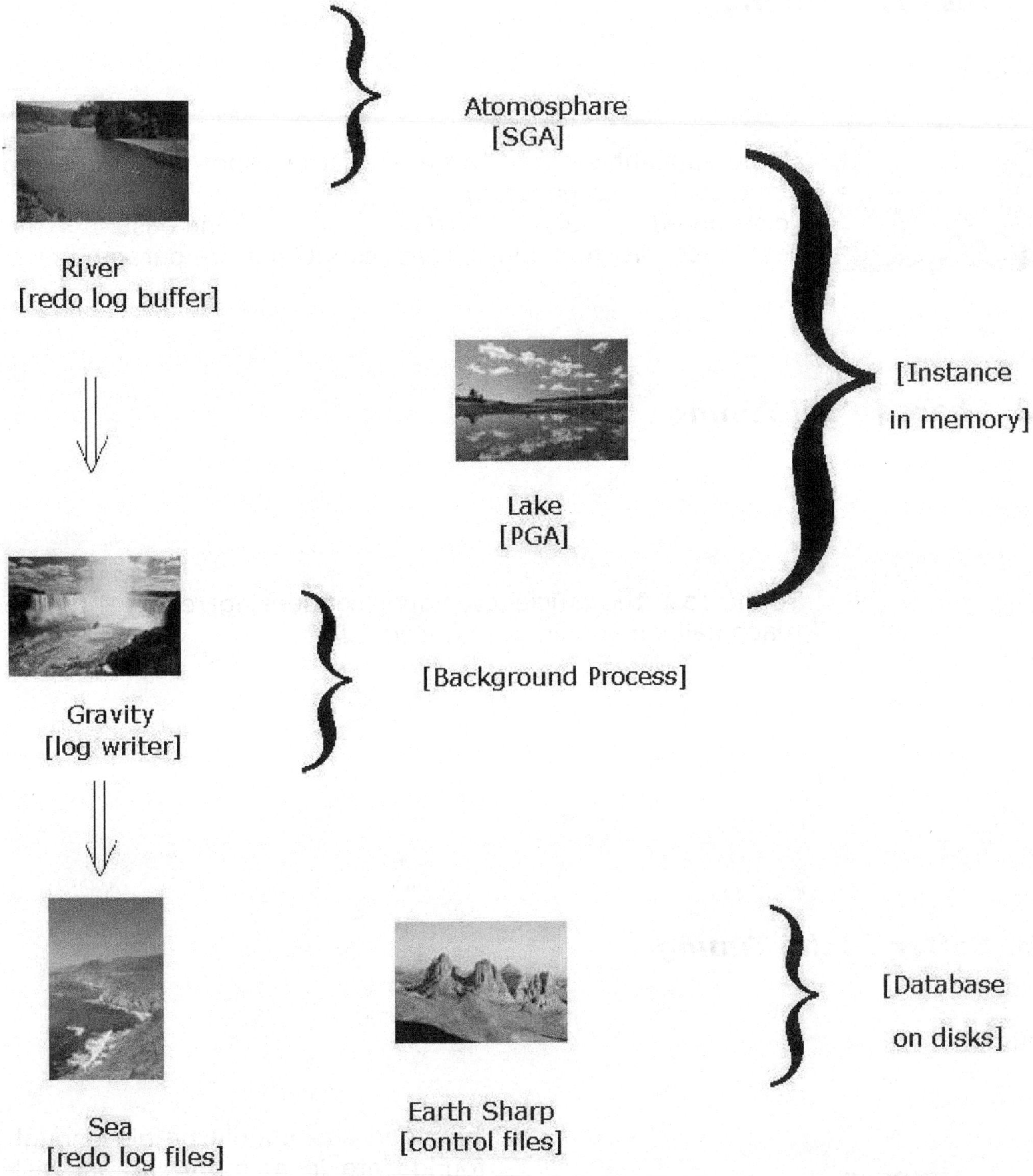
Atomosphare
[SGA]
River
[redo log buffer]
Lake
[PGA]
[Instance
in memory]
Gravity
[log writer]
[Background Process]
Sea
[redo log files]
Earth Sharp
[control files]
[Database
on disks]

### 6.1. Disk I/O Tuning

Sunlight:

If the sunlight covered more area, the vapor from ocean to cloud could be speeded up.
[distributed disk I/O and increase the "database_file_multiblock_read_count" init.ora parameter].

### 6.2. Shared Pool Tuning

Air:

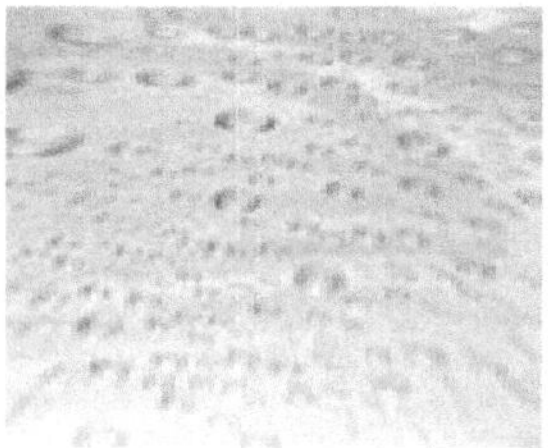

To increase the efficiency, vapor condensing[reparse] before reach balloon should be reduced.

### 6.3. Buffer Cache Tuning

Cloud:

⟹

The cloud size should be big enough [found data in memory without disk reading], and multiple layers of cloud could be setup [use multiple buffer pools: keep pool, recycle pool, default pool].

## 6.4. Database Writer Tuning

Rain:

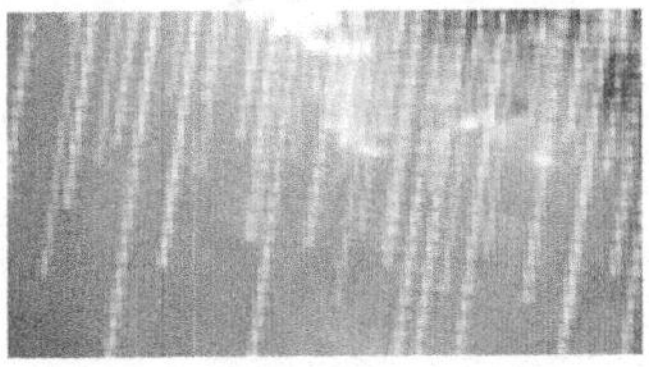

It would be more efficient if the rain[database writer] occurred in multiple locations [defined multiple database writer in "database_writer_processes" init.ora parameter]

## 6.5. Log Buffer Tuning

River:

Less dam should be built from river to sea to reduce obstruction. [No log buffer space waits and reduces contention to the log files]

## 6.6. Sorts Tuning

Ocean:

As moving in air faster than in water, therefore, make sure there was enough temporary storage in air [reduce disk read by enough temp space and make disk sorts/memory sorts < 5%].

## *6.7. Shared Server Tuning*

Balloon:

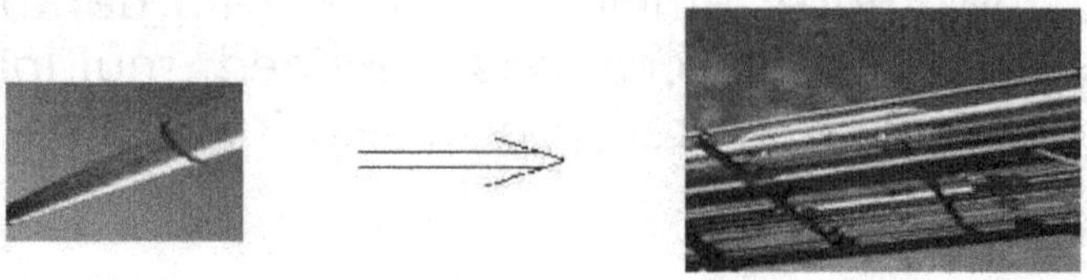

Multiple pipes could be used to speed up the extraction from vapor to balloon [add in more "dispatchers/shared_servers" init.ora parameters].

Well, although have so many ideas, which one among the above solutions needed to be applied?

Before any action taken, Fogg want to find out where is the actual bottleneck of slowness, and then only can he make decision.

# THE END

*Phileas Fogg had won his wager, and had made his journey around the world in eighty days. To do this he had employed every means of conveyance--steamers, railways, carriages, yachts, trading-vessels, sledges, elephants... The eccentric gentleman had throughout displayed all his marvellous qualities of coolness and exactitude. But what then? What had he really gained by all this trouble? What had he brought back from this long and weary journey?*

*Nothing, say you? Perhaps so; nothing but a charming woman, who, strange as it may appear, made him the happiest of men!*

*When the poet-king, Ucaf Uddaul, celebrates the charms of the queen of Ahmehnagara, he speaks thus:*

*"Her shining tresses, divided in two parts, encircle the harmonious contour of her white and delicate cheeks, brilliant in their glow and freshness. Her ebony brows have the form and charm of the bow of Kama, the god of love, and beneath her long silken lashes the purest reflections and a celestial light swim, as in the sacred lakes of Himalaya, in the black pupils of her great clear eyes. Her teeth, fine, equal, and white, glitter between her smiling lips like dewdrops in a passion-flower's half-enveloped breast. Her delicately formed ears, her vermilion hands, her little feet, curved and tender as the lotus-bud, glitter with the brilliancy of the loveliest pearls of Ceylon, the most dazzling diamonds of Golconda. Her narrow and supple waist, which a hand may clasp around, sets forth the outline of her rounded figure and the beauty of her bosom, where youth in its flower displays the wealth of its treasures; and beneath the silken folds of her tunic she seems to have been modelled in pure silver by the godlike hand of Vicvarcarma, the immortal sculptor."*

*– From Jules Verne, <<Around the World in 80 Days>>*

Made in the USA
Monee, IL
08 November 2026

67378668R00037